GLIMPSES OF GRACE

GLIMPSES OF GRACE

WORSHIP SERVICES BASED
ON WOMEN OF THE BIBLE

By
GLADYS C. MURRELL

ABINGDON PRESS
NEW YORK   ●   NASHVILLE

GLIMPSES OF GRACE

Copyright MCMXLI by Whitmore & Stone

Library of Congress Catalog Card Number: 41-25505

K

SET UP, PRINTED, AND BOUND BY THE
PARTHENON PRESS, AT NASHVILLE,
TENNESSEE, UNITED STATES OF AMERICA

1295186

We search the world for truth. We cull
The good, the true, the beautiful,
From graven stone and written scroll,
And all old flower-fields of the soul;
And, weary seekers of the best,
We come back laden from our quest,
To find that all the sages said
Is in the Book our mothers read.
—JOHN GREENLEAF WHITTIER

PREFACE

These worship services are designed for women's groups where there is need for a number of correlated services. The study of Bible women is a fascinating one. Unimportant as woman was considered to be in the early religious life of the human family, it is interesting to note how greatly she influenced it by her personality and her endowments.

The leader of the worship service will undoubtedly acquaint herself with the entire scripture story concerning the Bible woman chosen. In most cases, however, this would be too long to read to the average group for a devotional reading. In services where this is true, a scripture reading upon the theme is added for use.

Each meditation is written to stress the spiritual grace which is the theme of the service. Each grace may be a part of the Christian life of today.

It is my earnest prayer that the blessing I have received in preparing these services may be shared by those who shall use them.

—GLADYS C. MURRELL

ACKNOWLEDGMENTS

Sincere thanks are here expressed for the wisdom, truth, and beauty contributed by the poets and other writers whose thoughts are quoted in these services. In spite of all efforts, some of them remain unknown. Information as to their identity will be welcomed, and recognition will gladly be accorded in future editions.

Special acknowledgment is due to the following publishers and authors who have graciously given permission for use of the materials named:

To Abingdon-Cokesbury Press for "My Faith," from *Spiritual Hilltops* by Ralph S. Cushman; for "To Martha at Bethany: Spring 33 A.D." and "Not of Mary Alone," from *New Testament Women and Problems of Today* by Madeleine S. Miller; and for a prayer by Roy Price from *The Book of Daily Devotion* by Clark and Cram.

To D. Appleton-Century Company, authorized publisher, for lines by William Cullen Bryant.

To the Board of Christian Education of

the Presbyterian Church in the United
States of America for two stanzas from
the hymn by Calvin W. Laufer "We
Thank Thee, Lord, Thy Paths of Serv-
ice Lead," copyright 1919 by Calvin
W. Laufer.

To *The Christian Century* for the poem
"Recompense" by John Richard More-
land.

To W. B. Conkey Company for the poem
"Attainment" by Ella Wheeler Wilcox.

To Houghton Mifflin Company for the
poem "Courage" by Celia Thaxter; and
for lines by Lowell, Longfellow, and
Whittier.

To Little, Brown & Company for the
poems "Patriotism" and "A Single
Stitch," by Susan Coolidge.

To The Methodist Publishing House
(formerly the Methodist Book Con-
cern) for the poem "A Woman's Song
of Praise" by Ina Draper Defoe which
appeared in *The Senior Quarterly*.

To The Pilgrim Press for a prayer from
Prayers of the Social Awakening by

Walter Rauschenbusch. Copyright, The Pilgrim Press, and used by permission.

To Charles Scribner's Sons for the poem "Gradatim" by J. G. Holland.

To Charles K. Bolton for the poem "The Inevitable" by his mother, Sarah K. Bolton.

To Mary S. Edgar for the poem "The Upward Road."

To Maude White Hardie for the poem "Revelation."

To P. R. Hayward for lines from the poem "The Lure of the Unattained."

To Daniel Henderson for the poem "Hymn for a Household."

To the late John Oxenham for the poem "Credo."

To Loyal M. Thompson for the poem "Compensation."

CONTENTS

13

Abigail, the gracious

Honor to those whose words or deeds
Thus help us in our daily needs.
                    —HENRY W. LONGFELLOW

Abigail means "source of joy."
SCRIPTURE STORY: I Samuel 25:2-42.
SCRIPTURE READING: I Peter 4:7-10.
HYMN: "Walk in the Light."

MEDITATION:

Abigail was the wife of the churlish
Nabal, who was very rich in possessions.

After the manner of his time, David,
who was sojourning in Paran, claimed hospitality from Nabal and was refused with
insulting words.

When Abigail was told by one of the servants of this lack of courtesy, she was ap-
palled. Without Nabal's knowledge she
hastily collected a generous supply of food
and herself made the journey down to David's camp. David had armed his men and in
retaliation was about to take Nabal captive,

with all of his belongings, when he saw Abigail approaching. She tactfully apologized for her husband's stupidity and begged him to accept the food.

When Abigail arrived home, Nabal was holding a drunken feast with his shearers; so she did not mention her gifts to David that night. In the morning when she told him of her journey, Nabal seemed very ill, and he died several days afterward.

David had been much impressed by Abigail's beauty and gracious hospitality, and when he learned of her husband's death he asked her to become his wife.

PRAYER:

O God who knowest that we are not sufficient of ourselves but that all our sufficiency is of thee, help us in our work for others, direct us in thy wisdom, support us by thy power, that we may serve thee well and be good and profitable servants in thy kingdom. In Jesus' name. Amen.

BEAUTIFUL THINGS

Beautiful faces are those that wear—
It matters little if dark or fair—
Whole-souled honesty printed there.

Beautiful eyes are those that show,
Like crystal panes where hearthfires glow,
Beautiful thoughts that burn below.

Beautiful lips are those whose words
Leap from the heart like songs of birds,
Yet whose utterances prudence girds.

Beautiful hands are those that do
Work that is earnest and brave and true
Moment by moment the long day through.

Beautiful feet are those that go
On kindly ministries to and fro—
Down lowliest ways if God wills it so.

Beautiful shoulders are those that bear
Careless burdens of homely care
With patient grace and daily prayer.

Beautiful lives are those that bless—
Silent rivers of happiness,
Whose hidden fountain but few may guess.
—AUTHOR UNKNOWN

Anna, the devout

I have seen the face of Jesus
Tell me not of aught beside,
I have heard the voice of Jesus:
All my soul is satisfied!
—AUTHOR UNKNOWN

Anna means "grace, favored."
SCRIPTURE: Luke 2:22-39.
HYMN: "Faith of our Fathers."

MEDITATION:

Luke tells us about the saintly prophetess Anna, who had lived in the temple for eighty-four years, worshiping, fasting, and praying that she might see the coming of the Messiah. When she beheld the child Jesus being blessed by Simeon, she burst into rapture and proclaimed that she had seen the Lord. Her eyes were open to spiritual things and she recognized the Messiah.

PRAYER:

We thank thee, O God, with our whole hearts, and bless thy name forever and ever;

18

thou hast done all things well. We were in sorrow and saw no light; then thou hadst pity on us. We cried to thee in our trouble, and thou didst hear our voice; our cry entered into thine ears and thou didst comfort us. We will take the cup of salvation and call upon the name of the Lord. His praises shall be on our lips. Govern, guide, and lead us that we may daily grow in gratitude and love to thee, through thy Son, our Lord and Saviour Jesus Christ. Amen.

—B. ALBRECHT (A.D. 1589)

HIS CHOSEN ONES

Some souls there are, beloved of God,
Who, following where the saints have trod,
Learn such surrender of the will
They seem insensible of ill.

Yet, finely strung and sensitive,
They live far more than others live,
And grief's and pain's experience
Must be to them far more intense.

A mystery—that such can know
A life impregnable to woe!
O paradox that God alone
In secret proveth to his own!

GLIMPSES OF GRACE

It must be that supremest grace
So nerves them for the heavenly race
Their litanies are turned to psalms,
Their crosses, even here, to palms.

—HARRIET McEWEN KIMBALL

Asenath, the devoted

Not till the hours of light return
All we have built, do we discern.
—NATHAN ARNOLD

Asenath means "beauty."

SCRIPTURE STORY: Genesis 41:45; 46:20;
48:8-22; 50:22-26.

SCRIPTURE READING: Proverbs 1:7-9.

HYMN: "My Soul, Be on Thy Guard."

MEDITATION:

Asenath was born in Egypt, the daughter of Potipherah, a priest of On. On was the center of sun worship. Among the honors conferred by the Pharoah upon Joseph was the hand of Asenath in marriage. She became the mother of Manasseh and Ephraim. We find Jacob, the father of Joseph, adopting the two sons of Asenath into the clan to which Joseph belonged. We can picture Asenath becoming a true worshiper of Jehovah, adapting herself to the lives of her husband's people and letting her sons grow

21

up as Israelites, even though they lived in Egypt. We think of her as the faithful mother of sons whose generations have called her blessed.

We learn that Gideon and Jephtha descended from Manasseh, and Joshua, Deborah, Hannah, and Samuel claimed Ephraim as an ancestor.

PRAYER:

God of the ages, we come to thee today as women in a world enlightened by Christ, where we have a chance to know thee through him. We thank thee that thou dost send release from superstition, ignorance, and sin to those who believe and trust in his way of life. As we read of this woman of long ago, who worshiping thee found comfort and spiritual stamina, may we be fully mindful of our privileges and power today. We thank thee for everything. Amen.

ASENATH, THE DEVOTED

A WOMAN'S SONG OF PRAISE

I am a woman, singing as I go
About my work, hoping all the world may know
And love my song.   There is a humbleness in
    me
There is sometimes ecstasy,
Because I am alive.   I know
The loveliness of life and love.

I know that God is not above,
In some far heaven;
But here beside my path, with leaven
Of faith to lighten all my days.

I sing his praise,
Rejoicing that he made a world
Where all of beauty lies unfurled
For one who pauses and will listen
For the swish of unseen wings.

Ah! I need never sigh,
Knowing love and beauty cannot die.

—INA DRAPER DEFOE

Deborah, the leader

Ah then, my soul, bethink yourself,
For God has spread this scroll
To test the stuff of your rough hewn faith
And the fiber of your soul.
—Percy R. Hayward

Deborah means "bee, orderly motion."
Scripture Story: Judges 4 and 5.
Scripture Reading: Psalm 46:1-7.
Hymn: "Lead On, O King Eternal."

Meditation:

In the hill country of Ephraim there lived a remarkable woman who was a prophetess. Deborah received instructions from Jehovah, which she passed on to the Israelites. She sat under her own palm tree, and they came to her for judgment. This woman was known throughout the tribes, for they had been for two centuries without a prophet.

Deborah saw the misery of her people, who had no strong leadership to oppose the vigorous Sisera. She had a great faith that God would lead the Israelites to victory.

Calling Barak, she named him commander-in-chief of the armies and outlined for him a plan to save his people. When Barak hesitated, Deborah promised to go with the army. Through her a flood of faith poured into the dispirited warriors. Sisera himself met his death. The Canaanites were routed and every one killed. The account is a bloody one, but peace reigned for forty years afterward. Deborah's long life of devotion to her people was crowned by this victory. She holds a unique place among the women of the Old Testament. Her song in Judges 5 is claimed to be one of the best odes in the literature of the world.

PRAYER:

Help us to find thee, O God, in the hearts and lives of those about us. Let us help each other to be courageous and to plan our lives so that the greatest good may come to the largest number. Though we may be separated by prejudice, injustice, and circumstances, help us to be understanding; grant us patience and kindness that we may all together feel our relationship as chil-

dren of a wise and beneficent Father.
Amen.

GOD KNOWS

God knows—not I—the devious way
  Wherein my faltering feet may tread,
Before into the light of day,
  My steps from out this gloom are led,
And, since my Lord the path doth see,
What matter if 'tis hid from me?

God knows—not I—how sweet accord
  Shall grow at length from out this clash
Of earthly discords which have jarred
  On soul and sense; I hear the crash,
Yet feel and know that on his ear
Break harmony—full, deep, and clear.

He knoweth, too, despite my will
  I'm weak when I should be most strong.
And after earnest wrestling still
  I see the right yet do the wrong.
Is it that I may learn at length
Not mine, but his, the saving strength?

His perfect plan I may not grasp,
  Yet I can trust Love Infinite,
And with my feeble fingers clasp
  The hand which leads me into light.
My soul upon his errands goes,
The end I know not—but God knows.
                              —AUTHOR UNKNOWN

Dorcas, *the charitable*

A kindly act is a kernel sown
  That will grow to a goodly tree,
Shedding its fruit when time is flown
  Down the gulf of Eternity.
                    —JOHN B. O'REILLY

Dorcas means "gazelle, roe."
SCRIPTURE STORY: Acts 9:36-42.
SCRIPTURE READING: Psalm 41:1-3.
HYMNS: "A Charge to Keep I Have."
  "Take My Life, and Let It Be."
  "Go, Labor On!"

MEDITATION:

Dorcas is called "the woman who was always wanted." She was one who saw the need about her—sewing for those who had no clothes, cooking for those who had no food, and giving spiritual help to those who were comfortless. When she died, her friends could not bear her loss and stood about weeping. They wept not merely for the work of her hands, but because they missed her sympathetic and loving person-

27

ality. We rejoice that it was possible for Peter, used of God, to restore her to life.

Dorcas was the forerunner of those who today are doing social service without pay: the Woman's Society, the Service Guild, the benevolent committees of the church, the missionary societies, and all other women's organizations which serve the community and the world because of their love to Christ. The lives of these women entitle them to Christ's invitation: "Come, ye blessed of my Father, inherit the kingdom prepared for you from the foundation of the world: for I was hungry, and ye gave me to eat; I was thirsty, and ye gave me drink, I was a stranger, and ye took me in, naked, and ye clothed me; I was sick, and ye visited me; I was in prison, and ye came unto me."

SYMPATHY

Ask God to give thee skill
    In comfort's art,
That thou may'st consecrated be
    And set apart
Unto a life of sympathy,
For heavy is the weight of ill
    In every heart;

And comforters are needed much,
Of Christlike touch.
—A. E. HAMILTON

PRAYER:

O God of all—the poor, the weak, the needy, the sick and sore distressed—give us courage and zeal to do our self-assigned tasks in thy Kingdom. May we never lack the spiritual strength to take us victoriously through the strain of physical and mental labor. May we bless and benefit those with whom we come in contact. We know that thou wilt be with us even unto the end. Amen.

NOT LOST

The look of sympathy; the gentle word
Spoken so low that only angels heard;
The secret act of pure self-sacrifice,
Unseen by men, but marked by angels' eyes—
    These are not lost.

The kindly plans devised for others' good,
So seldom guessed, so little understood;
The quiet, steadfast love that strove to win
Some wanderer from the ways of sin—
    These are not lost.
—AUTHOR UNKNOWN

Elisabeth, the humble

Thy home is with the humble, Lord;
The simplest are the best,
Thy lodging is in childlike hearts;
Thou makest there thy rest.

—LYRA CATHOLICA

Elisabeth means "oath of God."
SCRIPTURE STORY: Luke 1:5-24, 39-45, 57-
80.
SCRIPTURE READING: Philippians 4:4-7.
HYMNS: "Take Time to Be Holy."
"Have Thine Own Way."

MEDITATION:

Elisabeth lived in the Judean hills with her husband, the priest Zacharias. Her tasks were probably many, as she undoubtedly cared for her husband's priestly vestments and belongings in addition to her own household duties.

For many years no child was born to Elisabeth and Zacharias; so their joy was great when a son was promised.

Shortly after this revelation Mary of Nazareth, Elisabeth's cousin, came to visit her. She found out that Mary had also had a vision, that she was to bear a son who was to be the Messiah. Elisabeth was deeply humble, saying, "And whence is this to me, that the mother of my Lord should come to me?"

Later Elisabeth taught her small son John reverence and humility. She must have passed on to him the story that Mary of Nazareth had told her during their visit together. For John greeted Jesus at the time of baptism with similar words: "I have need to be baptized of thee, and comest thou to me?"

After John left home, we hear no more of Elisabeth. She probably did not share his triumphs and defeats, but remained quietly at home; or, being an elderly woman when he was born, she may have died before he became a man.

However, our memory of Elisabeth is of a generous, humble woman who placed others before herself.

PRAYER:

> In humbleness, O Lord, I ask
> That thou bestow on me
> The will and strength to do some task
> For growth of love for thee;
> Some task, not of my chosen will—
> For wisdom is not mine—
> But let my poor frailsome life fulfill
> Some perfect thought of thine. Amen.
>
> —AUTHOR UNKNOWN

A SINGLE STITCH

One small life in God's great plan,
How futile it seems as the ages roll,
Do what it may or strive how it can
To alter the sweep of the infinite whole!
A single stitch in an endless web,
A drop in the ocean's flood and ebb!
But the pattern is rent where the stitch is lost,
Or marred where the tangled threads have
crossed;
And each life that fails of its true intent
Mars the perfect plan that its Master meant.

> —SUSAN COOLIDGE

Esther, the loyal

And he will touch the trembling lips with fire;
Oh, let us hasten, lest we come too late!
                                    —AUTHOR UNKNOWN

Esther means "happiness, star."
SCRIPTURE STORY: Book of Esther.
SCRIPTURE READING: Proverbs 22:1-6.
HYMN: "True-hearted, Whole-hearted."

MEDITATION:

Esther was chosen by King Ahasuerus of
Persia as the loveliest of the maidens who
were brought before him. She was a Jewess,
although her Hebrew blood was not mani-
fest in her appearance. Esther became his
queen and lived in royal luxury, beloved by
the monarch.

One day her uncle, Mordecai, came to her
to tell her that the king, influenced by
Haman, had ordered all the Jews in the
kingdom to be slaughtered. He asked her
intervention with the king, urging her with
these words, "Who knows whether thou art

33

not come to the kingdom for such a time as this?"

Esther promised to use her influence with Ahasuerus to save her people. Realizing that she might lose her life by coming before the king when he had not sent for her, Esther promised, "I go unto the king, and if I perish, I perish."

We remember how this brave queen arrayed herself in all her finery and appeared before the king, who granted her request, bringing about the salvation of the Jews and the downfall of Haman.

Esther has been proclaimed throughout the years as a woman who faced death to save her people. Her tomb in Hamadan, Iran, is honored and preserved even today.

PRAYER:

Our heavenly Father, may the loyal lives of others inspire us to sacrificial service. May we be true in times of our testing. We may not be subjected to great tests, where we may save our nation, but many times the welfare of our own family or community depends upon our right attitudes and willing service. Teach us to be kindly, understanding, and zealous for the right in our everyday lives. In Jesus' name. Amen.

PATRIOTISM

He serves his country best
Who lives pure life and doeth righteous deed,
And walks straight paths however others stray,
And leaves his sons, as uttermost bequest,
A stainless record which all men may read;
This is the better way.

No drop but serves the slowly lifting tide;
No dew but has an errand to some flower;
No smallest star but sheds some helpful ray,
And man by man, each helping all the rest,
Make the firm bulwark of the country's power;
There is no better way.

—SUSAN COOLIDGE

1295186

Hagar, the obedient

> A maid whom there were none to praise,
> And very few to love.
>   —WILLIAM WORDSWORTH

Hagar means "stranger, flight."

SCRIPTURE STORY: Genesis 16:1-16; 17:20;
   21:8-21.

SCRIPTURE READING: Psalm 39:12-13.

HYMN: "O Sometimes the Shadows Are
   Deep."

MEDITATION

Hagar was born in Egypt and taken away
into Canaan to be the servant of Sarah and
Abraham.

After Sarah's jealousy had caused Abraham to send Hagar away, the serving maid
and her little son Ishmael wandered south-
ward in the wilderness. There seemed to
be no hope for them but death from hunger
and thirst. Hagar's grief was so great at
seeing the suffering of her son that she
turned her face away. But as the child

moaned in his thirst, God spoke to her, causing her to find a spring of water which she had not seen before. They were soon revived and lived on food in the wilderness until Ishmael became a stalwart man. He learned archery through these hard years in Paran. Hagar helped him to find an Egyptian girl for his wife. The Mohammedans of today claim their descent from Ishmael.

RECOMPENSE

All that we say returns,
The bitter word or sweet;
Days, weeks, or years may intervene, but soon
   or late
The spoken word and speaker meet.

All that we do returns,
The deed that's true or base
We may forget, but all unseen and parallel
The doer and the deed keep pace.
                              —JOHN RICHARD MORELAND

PRAYER:

Almighty Father, for this day we give thee praise. With overshadowing love thou dost watch over thy children from one generation to another; amid all the circumstances of our daily lives thou dost preside. Graciously help us to abide in thee, that evermore we may be steadfast and strong. For the light that has never failed and the grace that has never left us in other days, for the hopes that have chastened our sorrow, we lift up our hearts to thee in praise and worship. May the coming days be filled with a high sense of the sacredness of the personalities of others and of the value of our time. May the numberless memories of thy untiring love deliver us from every crooked way, from every evil thought and imagination. Through Jesus Christ our Lord. Amen.

Hannah, the consecrated

The reason why we obtain no more in prayer is
because we expect no more. God usually answers
us according to our hearts.

—RICHARD ALLERNE

Hannah means "grace, prayer."

SCRIPTURE STORY: I Samuel 1:1-28; 2:
1-11, 18-21.

SCRIPTURE READING: Psalm 42:1-5.

HYMNS: "There's a Wideness in God's
Mercy."

"O Worship the King."

MEDITATION:

Hannah, the wife of Elkanan, was child-
less. There was no greater sorrow for an
oriental wife, than that of being denied
children. She prayed that she might have
a son, and promised that she would dedicate
him to God and the church, were her request
granted. When Samuel was born, she did
not forget her promise. As soon as Samuel
was old enough, she brought him to Eli, the

priest in Shiloh, for training. But she did not cease praying for her son. Every year when she went with her husband to the temple she brought him a new robe which she had made. The following scripture is the prayer song of Hannah as she presented Samuel to Eli the priest; I Samuel 2:1-10.

If every home were an altar
  Where harsh or angry thought
Were cast aside for a kindly one
  And true forgiveness sought,

If every home were an altar
  Where hearts weighed down with care
Could find sustaining strength and grace
  In sweet uplift of prayer,

Then solved would be earth's problems,
  Banished sin's curse and blight,
For God's own love would radiate
  From every altar light.

—AUTHOR UNKNOWN

PRAYER:

O God, since thou hast laid the little children into our arms in utter helplessness, with no protection save our love, we pray that the sweet appeal of their baby hands may not be in vain. May we who are mothers and fathers seek eagerly to join wisdom to our love, lest love itself be deadly when unguided by knowledge. If there are any who were blessed by love in their own infancy, but who have no child to whom they may give as they have received, grant them such largeness of sympathy that they may rejoice to pay their debt in full to all children who have need of them. Grant us great tenderness for all babes who suffer, and a growing sense of the divine mystery that is brooding in the soul of every child. For the sake of Christ, our Saviour. Amen.

—WALTER RAUSCHENBUSCH

Huldah, the wise

She openeth her mouth with wisdom;
And in her tongue is the law of kindness.
—Proverbs 31: 26

Huldah means "world."

Scripture Story: II Kings 22:14-20; II Chronicles 34:22-33.

Scripture Reading: Psalm 67:1-6.

Hymn: "Guide Me, O Thou Great Jehovah."

Meditation:

Following several bad kings, King Josiah of Judah was a righteous man. During his repairing of the temple the lost book of the law was discovered. When this was read to the king, he realized how far the people had digressed from it, and asked his priests to find someone to interpret what Jehovah would have him do. It is strange that they went to Huldah the prophetess, the wife of Shallum, as the chief religious authority of the time. However, during the years she

42

had kept her hold on Jehovah and knew his desires for his children, even though around her many followed other gods. She had hoped that sometime the Book of the Law might again be the guide of the king. She was ready with good advice, foretelling the destruction of the city, but promising safety and peace to Josiah.

PRAYER:

Dear Father God, we thank thee that thou art always ready to lead us into right decisions, if we but do our part. Forgive us for what we are, and help us to be what we might be. We have possibilities for daily growth in Christian living. Make us clear visioned that we may help others to see the way. May we be happy in our spiritual growth, and so lead others to the way of life. Amen.

ATTAINMENT

Use all your hidden forces. Do not miss
The purpose of this life, and do not wait
For circumstance to hold or change your fate.
In your own self lies destiny. Let this

GLIMPSES OF GRACE

Vast truth cast out all fear, all prejudice,
  All hesitation. Know that you are great,
  Great with divinity. So dominate
Environment, and enter into bliss.
Love largely and hate nothing. Hold no aim
  That does not chord with universal good.
    Hear what the voices of the silence say,
All joys are yours if you put forth your claim,
  Once let the spiritual laws be understood,
  Material things must answer and obey.
                    —Ella Wheeler Wilcox

Jehosheba, the protector

Standeth God within the shadow keeping watch
above his own.

—JAMES RUSSELL LOWELL

Jehosheba means "oath of God."

SCRIPTURE STORY: II Kings 11:1-20; 12:
1-16; II Chronicles 22:10-12.

SCRIPTURE READING: Psalm 48:9-14.

HYMN: "I Want a Principle Within."

MEDITATION:

Jehosheba was the daughter of King Jo-
ram and the sister of Ahaziah. When Ahaziah died, his mother Athaliah ordered all
the male descendants of her husband to be
destroyed and declared herself the queen.
Jehosheba loved her baby nephew Joash and
hid him away so that the bloodthirsty queen
did not find him. She concealed him for
six years in the house of Jehovah. Jehosheba
was undoubtedly responsible for the kind of
training the little Joash received.

There had been many wicked kings in

Israel, and the territory had been overrun by alien tribes. When Joash was seven years old, the priest Jehoiada made known the fact that a boy of royal blood was living. Joash was made king. With what pride Jehosheba must have watched the good king Joash as he repaired the temple of Jehovah. This brave woman will always be known for her deed.

PRAYER:

O Lord, grant to us so to love thee with all our heart, with all our mind, and all our soul, and our neighbor for thy sake; that the grace of charity and brotherly love may dwell in us, and all envy, harshness, and ill will may die in us; and fill our hearts with feelings of love, kindness, and compassion, so that, by constantly rejoicing in the happiness and good success of others, by sympathizing with them in their sorrows, and putting away all harsh judgments and envious thoughts, we may follow thee, who art thyself the true and perfect Love; through Jesus Christ our Lord. Amen.

—AUTHOR UNKNOWN

DUTY

Be thy duty high as angels' flight,
  Fulfill it, and higher will arise
Even from its ashes. Duty is infinite,
  Receding as the skies.
Were it not wisdom, then, to close our eyes
  On duties crowding only to appall?
No: Duty is our ladder to the skies;
  And climbing not, we fall.

—ROBERT LEIGHTON

Jochebed, the resourceful

She sees the Best that glimmers thro' the Worst,
She feels the sun is hid but for a night.
—ALFRED TENNYSON

Jochebed means "glory of God."

SCRIPTURE STORY: Exodus 2:1-10; 6:20;
7:7; Numbers 26:59.

SCRIPTURE READING: Psalm 37:1-4.

HYMNS: "O for a Faith That Will Not
Shrink."

"Faith of Our Fathers."

MEDITATION:

Jochebed was the wife of Amram of the
tribe of Levi. Her family with many other
Israelites were living in Egypt and were sub-
ject to the Pharaoh. Before her third child
was born, an edict went out over the country
that all male babies belonging to the Hebrews
should be killed at birth. Therefore she hid
her infant, Moses, as long as she could, and
then carefully made a covered basket and
placed him in the rushes on the river, where

the wealthy Egyptian women came to bathe. Miriam, the older sister, watched lest harm come to the baby; and when the Pharaoh's daughter discovered and adopted the chubby, loveable baby, she brought Jochebed, the child's own mother to nurse him. Jochebed had the exquisite pleasure of rearing her baby and instilling into him such love of race that Moses, with God's help, became the deliverer of his people.

Thus was a nation saved because of the resourcefulness of a mother.

PRAYER:

Dear Heavenly Father, may our love of little children fill us full of compassion for all peoples and races. As we think of thy great sacrifice for us and as we strive to comprehend more perfectly thy desires for all mankind, may we hold the welfare of all mothers' sons in our hearts. Going about our daily tasks, caring for our own families, may the spirit of peace and goodwill fill our hearts—

Lord God, who let your baby Son
    Pass earthward where his joys were few

To a hard death when all was done,
  And very far away from you,

Lord God, whose Son went steadily
  Down the hard road he had to tread,
Guard my son too, that he may be
  Strong in his hours of doubt and dread!
                                        Amen.
                          —HENRY WARD BEECHER

COURAGE

Because I hold it sinful to despond,
  And will not let the bitterness of life
Blind me with burning tears, but look beyond
  Its tumult and its strife;
Because I lift my head above the mist,
  Where the sun shines and the broad breezes
    blow,
By every ray and every raindrop kissed
  That God's love doth bestow;

Think you I find no bitterness at all?
  No burden to be borne, like Christian's pack?
Think you there are no ready tears to fall
  Because I keep them back?
Why should I hug life's ills with cold reserve,
  To curse myself and all who love me? Nay!
A thousand times more good than I deserve
  God gives me every day.
                          —CELIA THAXTER

Lydia, the convert

Whatever dies or is forgot,
Work done for God, it dieth not.
—THOMAS FRECKELTON

Lydia means "offspring."

SCRIPTURE STORY: Acts 16:14, 15, 40; Philippians 4:10-16.

SCRIPTURE READING: Philippians 3:8-12.

HYMNS: "Work, for the Night Is Coming." "Go, Labor On!"

MEDITATION:

Lydia had probably been born in the city of Thyatira, which was the center of the weaving and dyeing trade. The purple cloth of that section was eagerly sought by careful purchasers. She moved to Philippi, an important Macedonian city, where she imported this cloth and sold it. Business women were in a minority in her day, but she was keen and courageous and made a success of her work.

Lydia did not let business entirely engross

51

her, for she went regularly to meet with a group of women who prayed together. When Paul found them and preached to the group, she was converted to Christianity. Her experience was so satisfying that she won her whole household to Christ, and they were all baptized together. There was no church building; so she opened her home as a meeting place. She also entertained Paul and his friends when they were in Philippi. This church became one of the most helpful of the church Paul founded. In his letter to the Philippians, Paul is deeply appreciative of their zeal.

Lydia is known as the first Christian convert in Europe.

PRAYER:

Our Father, may our influence today be sweet and wholesome. May we inspire some faltering one by the confidence of our faith and the uprightness of our purpose. Pardon our misuse of thy gracious gift of speech. Help us to be ready ever to confess our faults and slow to publish our neighbor's failings.

Teach us the meaning of true service, and may thy presence illumine our minds and warm our hearts constantly.   Amen.

REVELATION

I seek no revelation from my God,
  No mystic seal, thunder, nor gleaming gold,
No flaming bush, still voice, nor budding rod.
  He who was thus revealed to men of old
To me speaks clear today.   For, when I see
  A life shine forth in service wholly his
A soul undaunted by adversity,
  Meeting earth's challenge and death's mys-
    teries
With steady calm, with wisdom and with grace
  No human logic can account for: then
I know this one has looked upon God's face
  And is his revelation here to men.
Clear visioned in this crystal light anew
I dare beseech, "Lord, speak through my life
    too!"

—MAUDE WHITE HARDIE

Martha, the practical

No service in itself is small;
None great, though earth it fill;
But that is small that seeks its own,
And great that seeks God's will.
　　　　　—Author Unknown

Martha means "mistress, lady."

Scripture Story: Luke 10:38-42; John
　11:1-11, 17-45; 12:1-8.

Scripture Reading: James 1:22-27.

Hymns: "Go, Labor On!"

"We May Not Climb the Heavenly
Steeps" (Immortal Love, Forever Full").

Meditation:

Martha lived in Bethany with her sister
Mary and her brother Lazarus. She was
very active. It may be she was one of those
who "cannot be helped" in the kitchen and
who likes to work alone. Perhaps she habit-
ually bore the burden of the housework because she felt she could do it better than
Mary.

Why was Martha fussy and unhappy in her work in the instance cited in Luke 10: 38-42? Was it because she did not pause for meditation and prayer before she began her tasks? She showed her spiritual insight when she said to the Master, "Yea Lord; I have believed that thou art the Christ, the Son of God, even he that cometh into the world." Did she straightway become so busy at her work that she lost sight of the real needs of Jesus?

Jesus knew that Martha, generous and capable though she was, put too much stress on small details and worried about things that did not matter. He had come, sorely in need of understanding and companionship, and appreciated Mary's attitude even more than the delicious food prepared by Martha.

Our guests in our home today come for fellowship as much as for food. Hospitality that is simple and kindly is more acceptable than a lavish spread served by an irritable, overworked hostess.

What secret trouble stirs thy heart?
  Why all this fret and flurry?
Dost thou not know that what is best
In this too restless world is rest
  From overwork and hurry?
            —HENRY W. LONGFELLOW

PRAYER:

O Lord, renew our spirits and draw our hearts unto thyself, that our work may not be a burden but a delight. Give us such a mighty love to thee as may sweeten all our obedience. May we serve thee with cheerfulness and gladness, and feel our burdens lightened by thy understanding and lovingkindness. Amen.

TO MARTHA AT BETHANY: SPRING 33 A.D.

Though menial are her tasks,
  No menial soul she brings
To their accomplishment;
  But joy within her sings,
For lo! the Guest who asks
  Her ministry has taught
How toil with meditation blent
  May be with vision fraught.
No longer cumbered, she, but thrilled

MARTHA, THE PRACTICAL

That his bright face has filled
The gloom of her small dwelling place
Again with his transforming grace.
She little dreams that on that kingly head,
　Which pensive Mary lavishly anoints,
While Lazarus ponders how he raised him, dead,
　Will soon be pressed dark Calvary's waiting
　　points.
Oh, come, Lord Jesus, knock again
And say wherever toiling men
And women feel their tasks a weight,
　My Father worketh even until now,
And I still work beside thee, dawn and late,
　And share with thee the drops upon thy
　　brow.

　　　　　　　　　　—MADELEINE S. MILLER

Mary of Bethany, the worshipful

Her eyes are homes of silent prayer.
—ALFRED TENNYSON

Mary means "bitterness, myrrh of the sea."

SCRIPTURE STORY: Matthew 26:6-14; Luke
10:38-42; John 11:1-45; 12:1-8.

SCRIPTURE READING: Romans 12:9-16.

HYMNS: "How Sweet the Name of Jesus
Sounds."

"More Like the Master."

PRAYER: (read) "O Master, Let Me Walk
with Thee."

MEDITATION:

The quiet desire of Mary of Bethany to
be near the Saviour, the spiritual nature
which caused her to perceive what others
did not see, may be difficult for us to understand today in this busy world. We are
apt to say pertly, "Yes, but where would the
world be if all of us were Marys?" Who
knows the answer to that? The women of
the world have never been all Marys.

People of her time did not understand her.

When Mary brought the pound of ointment of pure nard and anointed Jesus' feet—while Martha served dinner—the sentiment of the group was probably with Judas, who shouted, "Why was not this ointment sold and the money given to the poor?" Jesus' patient reproof quieted them, though still they wondered. But Mary's heart was happy. She had expressed her devotion in the lavish way she felt suitable to Jesus' kindness and love.

There are times when a tribute of pure love and sentiment is the richest thing in life. Most of us are so practical. We feel we must be. But let us sometimes give a sacrificial gift of pure love—some exquisite thing, even a perfect rose—but one that has cost us something. It purges our souls.

God's love hath in us wealth unheaped;
Only by giving is it reaped.
The body withers and the mind
Is pent up by a selfish rind.
Give strength, give thought, give deeds, give
    pelf,
Give love, give tears, and give thyself.
Give, give, be always giving,

Who gives not is not living;
The more we give
The more we live.

—AUTHOR UNKNOWN

PRAYER:

Father, we thank thee for the faithful
women who have blessed the world, whose
lives are radiant, who have followed Jesus
and generously lived for other's good. May
their pure and noble lives quicken and ani-
mate our hearts, and in our souls may there
burn a desire to become better Christians,
with the help of Christ our Lord. Amen.

MARTHA OR MARY?

I cannot choose; I should have liked so much
To sit at Jesus' feet—to feel the touch
Of his kind gentle hand upon my head
While drinking in the gracious words he said.

And yet to serve him—Oh, divine employ—
To minister and give the Master joy;
To bathe in coolest springs his weary feet,
And wait upon him while he sat at meat.

Worship or service—which? Ah, that is best
To which he calls us, be it toil or rest;
To labor for him in life's busy stir,
Or seek his feet, a silent worshiper.

—CAROLINE ATHERTON MASON

Mary of Jerusalem, the hospitable

> I am blest
> Only in what they share with me,
> In what I share with all the rest.

Mary means "bitterness, myrrh of the sea."

SCRIPTURE STORY: Acts 12:12; Romans 16:6.

SCRIPTURE READING: I Peter 3:14-18.

HYMNS: "How Firm a Foundation."
"Jesus Calls Us."

MEDITATION:

Mary, the mother of Mark was one of the best known of Jesus' followers. Hers was the home in Jerusalem with the "Upper Room." Jesus and his followers often met there, and it remained the meeting place for the early Christians as long as she lived.

She was related to two of the early followers of Christ's way of life. Mark, her son, was the devoted friend of Peter and the other disciples; and Barnabas, her nephew, was a faithful Christian. She perhaps also knew Paul, as these two young men were his companions on his first missionary journey.

We like to think that Mary's faith and knowledge aided Mark in writing the gospel record.

Mary's home was open to all Christians during a time of persecution. She was acquainted with the difficulties through which the disciples were passing.

PRAYER:

Lord Jesus, thou who hast been our Saviour through days which have gone by, be thou our Saviour and Leader today. Help us ever to be willing to minister to those who have bleeding hearts, bleeding bodies, or bleeding souls. Help us to see the distressed along the ways of life. We know that often we have seen the needs of the distressed, but have been unwilling to render service. O Jesus, help us to have a deeper interest in other people's needs. Help us to be more willing to serve those who have been wounded along the roads of life. Hasten the day when our interests will deepen for the broken-hearted, and be more anxious to feed the poor. Let desires so deepen in each of us that we will band together not only to make the wounded and hungry well and strong, but to clear the highways of thieves and robbers so that all peoples may travel life's highways unmolested and unafraid. Be thou our Leader this day, for we ask it in Christ's name. Amen.—ROY PRICE

STRENGTH FOR TODAY

Strength for today is all we need,
   As there never will be a tomorrow;
For tomorrow will prove but another today,
   With its measure of joy and sorrow.

Strength for today—what a precious boon
   For the earnest souls who labor,
For the willing hands that minister
   To the needy friend and neighbor.

Strength for today—that our precious youth
   May happily shun temptation,
And build, from the rise to the set of sun,
   On a strong and sure foundation.

Strength for today, in house and home,
   To practice forbearance sweetly;
To scatter kind deeds and loving word
   Still trusting in God completely.
               —AUTHOR UNKNOWN

Mary of Magdala, the grateful

> The Saviour calls for service;
> From your fears rise girt with faith.

Mary means "bitter, myrrh of the sea."
SCRIPTURE STORY: Luke 8:1-3; Mark 15:
40-41; John 20:1-18; Matthew 27:56.
SCRIPTURE READING: Ephesians 3:14-20.
HYMNS: "Amazing Grace."
"What a Friend We Have in Jesus."

MEDITATION:

Mary of Magdala had been cured by
Jesus from an acute nervous disorder and
showed her gratitude in many ways. Her
devotion caused her to follow him even to
the cross. She was the first to whom he
spoke after his resurrection. To her was
given the privilege of bearing the glad tid-
ings to his other disciples.

Jesus must have sensed many times this
deep gratitude of Mary and realized that
her humility and understanding would make
her receptive to his presence. We remember

64

that the disciples had difficulty in recognizing him, and that Thomas asked for proof that he was Jesus. But Mary knew his voice and answered him with the name "Rabboni," which was the most honorable title given to Jewish teachers.

We are glad that most students of the Bible do not link this Mary with the woman in Luke 7:36-50, believing that Mary of Magdala was not an immoral woman, but one who suffered from a severe illness from which she was cured by Christ. Be that as it may, we know that Jesus honored her in an unusual way and that after she was healed she was a most devoted follower of his way of life.

PRAYER:

O God, we thank thee for thy Son Jesus Christ, for his discernment, for his great power to overcome disease, sin, and ignorance. Wherever his spirit has gone in the world these blots have been removed. Help us to be instruments in his service that we may do our part in this great task. May we feel deep gratitude to those who have gone

on before inspired by thy grace and have
paved the way for a better world today.
For the sake of Jesus Christ. Amen.

NOT OF MARY ALONE

Not of Mary alone
  Asked Christ on Easter morn,
When death's cold sealing stone
  He burst with life newborn,
"Woman, why weepest thou?
Know ye not, I am risen now?"

But of every woman in Galilee
From Jordan's stream to the jeweled sea;
Of every woman by old laws bound
In temple and street where fetters ground,
In homes bereaved and courts oppressed,
He asked with voice which brought sweet rest;
"Woman, O woman, whom seekest thou?
Know ye not, I am risen now?"

Today he asks in the self same way
Of lives whom toil is wasting away
  In towns whose tasks no joys allow
For young hearts slain with hungering pain,
  "Woman, O woman, why weepest thou?
Can it be that I rose in vain?"

          —MADELEINE S. MILLER

Mary of Nazareth, the mother

She was with him, even unto the end.

Mary means "bitter, myrrh of the sea."

SCRIPTURE STORY: Matthew 1:18-25; Luke
  1:26-56; 2:1-52; John 2:2-11; 19:25-
  27.

SCRIPTURE READING: Luke 1:46-55.

HYMNS: "Silent Night."

"There's a Song in the Air."

MEDITATION:

The "Magnificat" in the first chapter of
Luke is Mary's song of joy and fulfillment.
It is sung at the happiest time of her life.

The annunciation of the angel, the beati-
tude of Elisabeth, the prediction of Zacharias, and the prophecies of Simeon and Anna
remained always in her mind; and surely she
pondered them often in her heart.

Some sadness and forboding must have
come into her heart, also, as she remembered
the old prophecies concerning the Messiah.
She was aware that they were not all joyous
predictions, but that he must also suffer.

Many questions which the tiny Jesus asked his mother must have been answered only after prayer. There must have been perfect understanding between Jesus and his mother.

Mary deliberately chose to be ignored and unnoted throughout the whole career of her son. But she followed him; and, watching him respond to his high mission, she was content. Some of his last words on the cross were about the care of his mother. Her humble words marveling at God's consideration of the "low estate of his handmaiden" were echoed later by Jesus when he said, "Whosoever would be great among you shall be your minister; and whosoever would be first among you shall be your servant."

COMPENSATION

She taught him as a little lad
    A lovely evening psalm.
He breathed its accents tenderly;
    It made his spirit calm.

And every youthful night he breathed,
    "My spirit I commend
Into thy loving Father care,"
    As to an earthly friend.

MARY OF NAZARETH, THE MOTHER

That mother on a lonely hill,
  Her son nailed to a tree—
The sword of pain had pierced her heart;
  Her lips moved tenderly.

Borne as a breath from childhood days,
  His words sweet comfort lend;
She heard, "Into my Father's hands
  My spirit I commend."

—LOYAL MORRIS THOMPSON

PRAYER:

Grant us, we beseech thee, almighty and
most merciful God, fervently to desire,
wisely to search out, and perfectly to fulfill all that is well-pleasing unto thee this
day. Order thou our worldly condition to
the glory of thy Name; and, of all that thou
requirest us to do, grant us the knowledge,
the desire, and the ability, that we may so
fulfill it as we ought; and may our path to
thee, we pray, be safe, straightforward, and
perfect to the end. Bestow upon us, also,
O Lord our God, understanding to know
thee, diligence to seek thee, wisdom to find
thee, and a faithfulness to follow thee,
through Jesus Christ our Lord. Amen.

—THOMAS AQUINAS (A.D. 1255)

Miriam, the enthusiastic

God gives each one a life, like a lamp, then gives
That lamp due measure of oil;
Lamp lighted—hold high, wave wide
Its comfort for others to share.

—MULEYKEH

Miriam means "exalted, rebellion."
SCRIPTURE STORY: Exodus 2:1-10; 15:20-
21; Numbers 12:1-15; 20:1.
SCRIPTURE READING: Psalm 66:1-7.
HYMN: "He Leadeth Me."

MEDITATION:

Miriam, the older sister of Moses, guarded
him as he lay in his basket in the reeds of
the river. She rushed to secure her mother
as nurse when Pharaoh's daughter adopted
him.

Miriam later led the music and festive
dancing to honor Moses' triumphs as leader
of the Israelites. She became known as a
prophetess and was honored by her people.

It is recorded that only once did she rebel
against her younger brother's authority. She

was saved from punishment for this because of Moses' intercession with God. Miriam did not enter the promised land but died in the desert of Zin at Kadesh and was buried there.

We have here the picture of an impetuous, loving woman, who, although not always right in her decisions, supplied enthusiasm and leadership during the difficult time when the Israelites were in the wilderness.

PRAYER:

Help us to be enthusiastic workers in thy Kingdom, O Lord. We pray for the courage to face problems of personal life, the facts which are thrust upon us, and to atone fully for our blunders and wrong decisions. Give us poise and self-control that we may not become the victims of our circumstances but that we may know the joy of victory.

We do not know what a day may bring forth. May we accept with faith what thou dost send and enter into each adventure with an enthusiastic optimism that does not know defeat. And finally as we come

to our last earthly day may our faith be
unperturbed as we enter into that which
thou hast prepared for them that love thee.
Amen.

GRADATIM

We hope, we resolve, we aspire, we pray,
And we think that we mount the air on wings,
Beyond the recall of sensual things,
While our feet still cling to the heavy clay.

Wings for the angels, but feet for men!
We may borrow the wings to find the way;
We may hope, and resolve, and aspire, and pray;
But our feet must rise, or we fall again.

Heaven is not reached at a single bound;
But we build the ladder by which we rise
From the lowly earth to the vaulted skies,
And we mount to its summit round by round.
—J. G. HOLLAND

Naomi, the adviser

Open the door of your heart, my lass,
  To the things that shall abide;
To the holy thoughts that lift your soul
  Like the stars at eventide.
                    —EDWARD EVERETT HALE

Naomi means "pleasantness."
SCRIPTURE STORY: Book of Ruth.
SCRIPTURE READING: Proverbs 22:17-21.

MEDITATION:

Naomi and her husband Elimelech with their two sons left Bethlehem and sought a home in Moab during the famine in their own country. Their sons, Chilion and Mahlon, married Orpah and Ruth of the country of Moab, and they all lived happily together for several years. However, after a time, the three women were left widows.

The famine being over in her home country, Naomi decided to go back to Bethlehem. She advised her daughters-in-law to remain in Moab. Orpah consented, but Ruth had lived in the same home with Naomi long enough to depend upon her counsel. She had learned to worship Jehovah and was willing to follow her mother-in-law to a strange country. With words that have echoed down the corridors of time (Ruth 1:16-17) this loyal daughter-in-law cast her lot with Naomi. From that time, the older woman accepted responsibility for the girl and continually advised her as to her conduct in the strange country.

Ruth, the beautiful foreigner, found favor in the eyes of Boaz, the wealthy owner of the field wherein she gleaned. Naomi carefully counseled Ruth as to customs in Bethlehem, and the girl willingly did as she was told. Her sweet pliable nature made her a charming and faithful wife to Boaz, whose happiness was complete at the birth of his son Obed. Naomi's joy, too, was great when she held in her arms the son of Ruth and Boaz, her kinsman. According to the custom, this child would be considered her own grandchild.

PRAYER:

Our Father and God, we are grateful for

74

this wise counselor of an ancient day. We realize that an older friend can be a blessing to us many times. We thank thee for all Christian women who have had the faith and vision to make a dark way bright and an obscure path plain for someone momentarily bewildered. Help each one of us to accept the responsibility of aiding youth to find its way in a kindly, patient, and understanding manner. May we be worthy to be called wise counselors and true disciples of thine. Bless our endeavors and bless those who look to us for guidance, that we may not fail thee or them. In Jesus' name. Amen.

We cannot make bargains for blisses,
    Nor catch them like fishes in nets;
And sometimes the thing our life misses
    Helps more than the thing which it gets.
For good lieth not in pursuing,
    Nor gaining of great nor of small,
But just in the doing, and doing
    As we would be done by is all.

—ALICE CARY

Nehushta, the courageous

If sorrow never claimed our heart,
And every wish were granted,
Patience would die and hope depart;
Life would be disenchanted.
—Author Unknown

Nehushta means "brazen fetter."
Scripture Story: II Kings 24:8-17; 25:
27-30; Jeremiah 29:1-7.
Scripture Reading: Psalm 137:1-6.
Hymn: "Be Strong."

Meditation:

Nehushta was the daughter of Elnathan
of Jerusalem. She married Jehoiakim, a son
of King Josiah, and lived in the royal palace
at Jerusalem for twenty years. Her son
Jehoiachin began to reign when he was eigh-
teen years of age and had reigned for eight
years when Nebuchadnezzar, the King of
Babylon, came against the city and took all
prisoner. The journey of eight hundred
miles from Jerusalem to Babylonia was a
weary one for the exiles on foot. For three

76

months Nehushta, the queen mother, with other women of the court was driven along the road toward a new and unfamiliar country. They missed the opportunity and place to worship. All was strange, though beautiful. How difficult they found it to be happy in a foreign land. Psalm 137 sings of their sorrow.

But Jeremiah the prophet, who remained in Jerusalem, sent a message to the exiled colony saying, "Build ye houses, and dwell in them; and plant gardens, and eat the fruit of them. Take ye wives, and beget sons and daughters . . . . and seek the peace of the city . . . . and pray unto the Lord for it." The women busied themselves, doubtless under the leadership of Nehushta. Her son Jehoiachin, who had been a bad king in Jerusalem, redeemed himself and winning the favor of the Babylonian king, was honored by him.

Since the Hebrews did not have their own temples in this foreign land, they observed more carefully the worship and reading of the sacred scrolls in their homes. Thus their

faith in Jehovah was strengthened, even in
sorrow and in exile.

THE INEVITABLE

I like the man who faces what he must
    With step triumphant and a heart of cheer;
    Who fights the daily battle without fear;
Sees his hopes fail, yet keeps unfaltering trust
That God is God; that somehow, true and just
    His plans work out for mortals; not a tear
    Is shed when fortune, which the world holds
        dear,
Falls from his grasp; better, with love, a crust
Than living in dishonor; envies not,
    Nor loses faith in man; but does his best
Nor ever mourns over his humbler lot,
    But with a smile and words of hope, gives zest
To every toiler; he alone is great
Who by life heroic conquers fate.

                —SARAH K. BOLTON

PRAYER:

May the power of the Father govern us.

May the wisdom of the Son enlighten us.

May the operation of the Holy Spirit quick-
en us.

O God, we beseech thee guard our souls;
    sustain our bodies, direct our course; bless

our undertakings; inspire us with holy
thoughts; pardon what is past; rectify
what is present; order what is to come;
and all for the sake of the Kingdom of
Jesus Christ, our Lord and Saviour.
Amen.—BISHOP ANDREWS (A.D. 1555)

Phoebe, the guest

May every soul that touches mine—
Be it the slightest contact—get therefrom some good.
Some little grace, or kindly thought,
One inspiration yet unfelt, one bit of courage
For the darkening sky, one gleam of faith
To brave the thickening ills of life.

—AUTHOR UNKNOWN

Phoebe means "chaste."
SCRIPTURE: Romans 16:1-2.
HYMNS: "Blest Be the Tie That Binds."
   "We Gather Together to Ask the Lord's
    Blessing."

MEDITATION:

Phoebe was a Christian matron living in
the eastern part of Corinth. She was probably a widow, as she was able to travel alone
to Rome. She was undoubtedly wealthy, as
she was referred to by Paul as a helper of
many. Knowing the bond between Christians, Paul sent a letter to the church at
Rome, introducing Phoebe.

We can imagine that she was received warmly and brought welcome news of Paul and the church at Cenchreae, near Corinth. She may have come on business of her own or on a mission for the church. Though far from home, we picture her as an honored guest as long as she stayed with the church in Rome.

There is a Power whose care
Teaches thy way along that pathless coast—
The desert and illimitable air—
    Lone wandering, but not lost.

He who, from zone to zone,
Guides through the boundless sky thy certain
        flight,
In the long way that I must tread alone,
    Will lead my steps aright.
                    —WILLIAM CULLEN BRYANT

PRAYER:

O God, our Father, we pray that thou wilt bind us closer together as sisters, in a deep and spiritual kinship. May we never see a stranger in our midst, but a sister working with us in thy vineyard. Teach

us how to be appreciative of each other, how
to see the best in others. May we remember
that we belong to thy great family, and may
we so live that we may enrich and bless the
lives of each other. Amen.

> Jesus united by thy grace,
>   And each to each endeared,
> With confidence we seek thy face,
>   And know our prayer is heard.
>
> Still let us own our common Lord
>   And bear thine easy yoke;
> A band of love, a threefold cord,
>   Which never can be broke.
>
> Touched by the loadstone of thy love,
>   Let all our hearts agree,
> And ever toward each other move,
>   And ever move toward thee.
>   —CHARLES WESLEY

Priscilla, the teacher

Jesus spoke to her as she plied her task.

Priscilla means "old, ancient."
SCRIPTURE STORY: Romans 16:3-5; Acts
   18:1-4, 24-28; I Corinthians 16:19; II
   Timothy 4:19.
SCRIPTURE READING: II Corinthians 4: 1-5.
HYMNS: "He Leadeth Me."
   "Wonderful Words of Life."

MEDITATION:

We know that Priscilla and her husband
Aquila were close friends of Paul in Rome.
She is mentioned several times in Paul's let-
ters, and her name is placed before that of
Aquila. This Christian couple was banished
from Rome when Claudius ordered the Jews
to leave. They were tentmakers and doubtless plied their trade in their home. They
were in Corinth and Ephesus with Paul,
whom we believe lived with them and also
worked at this trade.

Priscilla was probably the first woman

teacher of Christian theology. She found young and promising Apollos, who wished to preach, and helped him to understand Christ. He became so eloquent and so sure of himself that at times he seemed to rival Paul in popularity.

In Priscilla we have the unusual combination of homemaker, business woman, and teacher in the early Christian church where women were not recognized—a modern woman in an ancient day.

PRAYER:

Father, who hast furnished all things from thy great bounty, we ask thy help in the press of everyday duties. May we never be too busy to give thee a portion of each day. Thus our burdens will also be shared and our load made easier to bear.

Send thy spirit richly on all members of this group. Help each one of us to be an instrument in thy hands for good. Strengthen our minds and bodies; purify our hearts and fill us with love. Let no pride, dispute, or unkind words be known among us. Help us to be true and wise; and may thy peace rest upon us today and all our days, sweetening our trials and cheering us in our work together. In Jesus' name. Amen.

MY FAITH

I want the faith
That envies not
The passing of the days;
That sees all times and ways
More endless than the stars;
That looks at life,
Not as a little day
Of heat and strife,
But one eternal revel of delight
With God, the friend, adventurer, and light.
What matter if one chapter nears the end?
What matter if the silver deck the brow?
Chanting I go
Past crimson flaming
From the autumn hills,
Past winter's snow,
To find that glad new chapter
Where God's spring
Shall lift its everlasting voice to sing.
This is the faith I seek;
It shall be mine,
A faith that strides across the peaks of time!

—RALPH S. CUSHMAN

Rachel, the beloved

For though sometimes grief follows in its wake,
Still we forget love's sorrow in love's joy,
And cherish tears with smiles for love's dear sake;
Only in heaven is bliss without alloy,
   Thank God for love!

—AUTHOR UNKNOWN

Rachel means "serene, meek."
SCRIPTURE STORY: Genesis 29:1-35; 30:1-
   8, 22-24; 33:1, 2; 35: 16-20.
SCRIPTURE READING: Psalm 78:1-8.

MEDITATION:

As we read the ancient story of Rachel and Jacob, we are impressed again with the fact that God has to work through the people of the earth, imperfect though they be.

Jacob, on leaving home, went to the former dwelling-place of his mother, Rebekah, and fell in love with his cousin Rachel. Laban, her father, tricked him into working fourteen years for her hand in marriage, by giving him Leah, the elder daughter, at the end of the first seven years. During their married life, we find Jacob favoring Rachel and protecting her and her son Joseph when the tribe is in danger. Rachel died when her son Benjamin was born and was buried under a stone marker where her reputed tomb still exists today on the outskirts of Bethlehem. Jacob remembered her on his deathbed afterwards and gave his special blessing to her son Joseph (Genesis 49:22-26).

The story of Jacob's family is one of intrigue and trickery, but throughout we feel the deep devotion of Rachel and Jacob to each other. Jehovah seems to be able to work through this family, to bring his chosen people intact out of the time when there was much intermingling of races. Joseph, the son of Jacob and Rachel, was of pure Hebrew blood and the well-favored child of a happy and loving marriage.

PRAYER:

Our Heavenly Father, who dost work through thy imperfect children, we thank thee that thy divine touch is placed upon us.

We are grateful that thou dost "make the wrath of men to praise thee." Our mistakes are often turned by thee to some good. Wilt thou guide us and help us to follow thy will more perfectly and honestly. Show us thy plan for us and graciously lead us in the paths of kindliness, faith, and love. Through Jesus Christ our Lord. Amen.

MEN TOLD ME, LORD

I ask for nothing! Let the balance fall!
All that I am or know, or may confess
But swells the weight of my indebtedness;
Burdens and sorrows stand transfigured all;
Thy hands rude buffet turns to a caress,
For love, with all the rest, thou gavest me here,
And love is heaven's very atmosphere.
Lo, I have dwelt with thee, Lord! Let me die:
I could no more through all eternity!

—DAVID STARR JORDAN

Rebekah, the beautiful

But even beauty, howe'er blent
    To ear and eye, fails to content.
Only the heart, with love afire,
    Can satisfy the soul's desire.
                    —JAMES TERRY WHITE

Rebekah means "fettering by beauty."

SCRIPTURE STORY: Genesis 24:1-67; 25:
    19-34; 27:1-46; 28:1-5.

SCRIPTURE READING: Psalm 19.

HYMNS: "Yield Not to Temptation."
    "God of Grace and God of Glory."

MEDITATION:

Abraham sent his chief servant to Mesopotamia—where his brothers Nahor and Haran had gone—to seek a wife of his own kindred for his beloved son Isaac. The girl Rebekah was young, beautiful, and well trained in the courtesies of her time. She was one of a large household and a great-granddaughter of Nahor. She was chosen by the servant of Abraham, and with her personal attendants only she left her family

to go to a far country. She was never to
see her people again.

Twin sons, Esau and Jacob, were born to
the union of Isaac and Rebekah. Esau, the
first born, was a strange looking boy, while
Jacob was like her family. So she loved him
best. Equipped with the promise recorded
in Genesis 25:23, she trained Jacob for
leadership and helped him maneuver to get
the blessing of his sick father.

Later she paid the price of this favoritism
when she sent him back to her people that
he might escape the wrath of Esau. She
never saw her beloved son again. Isaac
probably outlived Rebekah.

> It is not just as we take it,
>   This mystical world of ours
> Life's field will yield as we make it
>   A harvest of thorns or of flowers.
>   —GOETHE

PRAYER:

Our Father and God, who dost give us
the commandments of the law to consist in
love toward God and toward man, grant

that we may so love thee and follow thy laws
that all envy, harshness, and ill will may die
in us. Fill our hearts with compassion,
love, and kindness that we may rejoice in the
success of others, sympathize with them in
sorrow, and refrain from harsh judgment at
all times. Through Jesus Christ. Amen.

A PRAYER FOR INSPIRATION

The prayers I make will then be sweet indeed,
    If thou the spirit give by which I pray;
    My unassisted heart is barren clay,
Which of its native self can nothing feed;
Of good and pious works thou art the seed
    Which quickens where thou sayst it may;
    Unless thou show us then thine own true way,
No one can find it! Father, thou must lead!
Do thou, then, breathe those thoughts into my
        mind
    By which such virtue may in me be bred
    That in thy holy footsteps I may tread;
The fetters of my tongue do thou unbind,
    That I may have the power to sing of thee,
    And sound thy praises everlastingly.
                    —MICHELANGELO BUONARROTI
            Translated by WILLIAM WORDSWORTH

Rhoda, the dependable

And God, who studies each separate soul,
Out of commonplace lives makes his beautiful whole.
—AUTHOR UNKNOWN

Rhoda means "rose."

SCRIPTURE: Acts 12:12-17.

HYMNS: "I Would Be True."

"True-hearted, Whole-hearted."

MEDITATION:

Rhoda was a little bondservant in the home of Mary, the mother of Mark, in Jerusalem. In this house was the "Upper Room," where Jesus and his disciples met when in the city.

Rhoda was a girl to be trusted and was assigned to the office of "keeper of the door." This required tact and wisdom. At this time the church of Jesus Christ was being established and there were many upper room conferences. Rhoda answered all knocks at the door, admitted messengers, missionaries, teachers, disciples, and persecuted Christians. Sometimes even agents of the Sanhedrin knocked to gain entrance, in order to trap some Christian.

There was a little window in the door which she opened, to learn who was knocking. She ran to ask her mistress when she was not sure of the welcome of the stranger.

One night, which she never forgot, she heard a knock. She could not see, but the voice said, "It is I, Peter."

Only that day she had been told that Peter was confined in a dungeon and guarded by soldiers to whom he was chained. All day Christians had been praying for him. Bewildered, she ran quickly to the upper room; and when she told the disciples, they could not believe her. They went with her to the door and in amazement beheld Peter, who had been delivered out of prison in a miraculous way. Thus the name of Rhoda is preserved for us through two thousand years.

PRAYER:

Our Heavenly Father, we thank thee for the strength that comes from thee.

Help us to be self-reliant, dependable, and courageous.

Wilt thou care for all of those who have been thrust out of the world of childhood into positions where loads are too heavy to bear. Bless all the young people of today, where great responsibility rests upon slender shoulders. May they be strong and true in their lives, and may they have the promise of better days. Through the Spirit of Jesus. Amen.

We thank thee, Lord, thy paths of service lead
To blazoned heights and down the slopes of
    need;
They reach thy throne, encompass land and sea,
And he who journeys in them walks with thee.

We've seen thy glory like a mantle spread
O'er hill and dale in saffron flame and red;
But in the eyes of men, redeemed and free,
A splendor greater yet while serving thee.
              —CALVIN W. LAUFER

Ruth, the faithful

All the strength of the world, and all its beauty, all true joy, everything that consoles, that feeds hope or throws a ray of light along our dark paths, comes to us from people of simplicity, those who have understood that the art of living is to know how to give one's life.

—CHARLES WAGNER

Ruth means "friend, looked upon with de·light."

SCRIPTURE STORY: Book of Ruth.

SCRIPTURE READING: Ruth 1: 16-17.

HYMN: "Bringing in the Sheaves."

MEDITATION:

Ruth, the Moabitess, left her own people to go to Bethlehem with her mother-in-law Naomi after the death of their husbands. It was at the beginning of the barley harvest when they reached Naomi's home country. Ruth found food for them by gleaning in the field of Boaz, a wealthy farmer. He had a responsibility toward them because of his relationship with Naomi's husband. Ruth's

95

charm and her devotion to her mother-in-law made the duty of Boaz a pleasure, and she later became his wife.

Most of the early Hebrew women led simple industrious lives. In all Oriental countries, however, the position of an unmarried woman or a young widow is unfortunate. She was even more unprotected in the ancient world, and only in the house of a husband could she find safety, respect, and rest.

Ruth through her loyalty to Naomi reaped the reward which every woman craved—the protection of a husband, a comfortable home, and children to carry on her husband's name.

PRAYER:

Dear Father, we know that thou wilt guide all who put their trust in thee. Come to our aid in hours of temptation that we may be loyal to our friends, to our family, and to the standards thou hast set for us. May every day bring triumph over fear, greed, and disloyalty in our lives and in the

world. Make us at peace with all mankind,
gentle to those who offend, faithful in all
duties, patient in distress, and ever thankful
for thy divine power which blesses us daily.
Amen.

"A commonplace life," we say, and we sigh;
  But why should we sigh as we say?
The commonplace sun in the commonplace sky
  Makes up the commonplace day.
The moon and the stars are commonplace things,
And the flower that blooms and the bird that
    sings
But dark were the world and sad our lot
If the flowers failed and the sun shone not;
For God, who studies each separate soul
Out of commonplace lives makes his beautiful
    whole.
                              —AUTHOR UNKNOWN

Salome, the ambitious

Whose aim is his own happiness is bad;
Whose aim is the good opinion of others is weak;
Whose aim is the happiness of others is virtuous;
Whose aim is God is great.

—TOLSTOY

Salome means "peaceable, reward."

SCRIPTURE STORY: Matthew 4:21-22; 20: 20-28; 27:56; Mark 15:40; 16:1.

SCRIPTURE READING: Matthew 20:25-28.

HYMNS: "O Jesus, I Have Promised."

"Jesus Calls Us."

MEDITATION:

Salome was the wife of Zebedee of Bethsaida. Her two sons James and John were called by Jesus to be his disciples. Doubtless Salome was often with the group of women who received inspiration and guidance from the Master.

Some students say that she was a sister of Mary the mother of Jesus. However, when Salome asked that her sons be given the chief places in Jesus' kingdom, she doubtless was thinking of honor rather than of service. Undoubtedly those present did not understand Jesus' meaning when he said, "Are ye able to drink the cup that I am about to drink?" "We are able," James and John answered. Then Jesus said, "The cup that I drink ye shall drink, but to sit on my right hand or on my left is not mine to give."

During the years following Jesus' death, James and John were tested many times. James was one of the first Christian martyrs. John, the beloved disciple, together with Salome, cared for Mary the mother of Jesus until she died.

We find Salome not only at the scene of the crucifixion but also at the tomb on resurrection morning. She was one of the few of Jesus' followers whose devotion carried her to hard places that she might minister to him.

CREDO

Not what, but whom, I do believe!
That, in my darkest hour of need,
Hath comfort that no mortal creed

To mortal man may give.
Not what, but whom!
  For Christ is more than all the creeds,
  And his full life of gentle deeds
  Shall all the creeds outlive.
Not what I do believe, but Whom!
  Who walks beside me in the gloom?
  Who shares the burden wearisome?
  Who all the dim way doth illume,
  And bids me look beyond the tomb
  The larger life to live?
Not what I do believe, but Whom!
Not what, but Whom!

—JOHN OXENHAM.

PRAYER:

O God, whose Spirit searcheth all things, and whose love beareth all things, we draw near thee in sincerity and truth. Enable us to sense thy love which hath forgiven us for our lack of understanding and to acknowledge our dependence upon thee for inspiration and guidance. May we have the grace of gratitude as we daily reap the blessings of Christianity in the world. Amen.

Sarah, the industrious

She looketh well to the ways of her household,
And eateth not the bread of idleness.
—PROVERBS 31: 27

Sarah means "princess."
SCRIPTURE STORY: Genesis 16:1-6; 17:15-
21; 23:1, 2, 19, 20.
SCRIPTURE READING: Proverbs 31:10-31.
HYMN: "A Charge to Keep I Have."

MEDITATION:

Sarah lived in a time when the family law
was the highest law. She and her husband
Abraham were nomads wandering from Ur
of Chaldea to Haran, to Egypt, and to Canaan. They lived in tents, and their wealth
lay in their herds. The family of Abraham
was composed of all of his blood relations,
his servants, and those who wished his protection. His power was absolute over those
in his family. Sarah as the mistress of this

household was doubtless very busy planning for the welfare of its members. She was gracious, hospitable, and beloved by her husband, who deferred to her judgment many times.

It is difficult for us to picture the living conditions in Sarah's day. She must superintend the grinding of grain into meal, the baking without an oven, the providing of clothing for the family, the carrying of the water, the quartering of the family and constant guests, the caring for provisions, and the nursing of the sick. Undoubtedly she was able to meet emergencies with calmness and resourcefulness. The camp was changed many times to find fresh pasturage for the herds, and each time this wife must settle her household comfortably and efficiently. We may well admire Sarah, the industrious, whose husband loved her so much that when after many years, she died, he bought her a tomb at Hebron. She was the first Hebrew woman to be buried thus. Abraham later was buried there with her.

SARAH, THE INDUSTRIOUS

HYMN FOR THE HOUSEHOLD

Lord Christ, beneath thy starry dome
We light this flickering lamp of home,
And where bewildering shadows throng
Uplift our prayer and evensong.
Dost thou, with heaven in thy ken,
Seek still a dwelling-place with men
Wandering the world in ceaseless quest?
O Man of Nazareth, be our guest!

Lord Christ, the bird his nest has found,
The fox is sheltered in his ground,
But dost thou still this dark earth tread
And have no place to lay thy head?
Shepherd of mortals, here behold
A little flock, a wayside fold,
That wait thy presence to be blest—
O Man of Nazareth, be our guest!
—DANIEL HENDERSON

PRAYER:

O God and Father of us all, we thank
thee for the progress the race has made. We
are grateful for thy leadership through the
centuries. Help us in this modern world to
serve thee efficiently and wisely and to minister to our household with Christian grace.

Remove the burdens from our hearts, and

relieve the anxieties of our minds. Forgive
the vain purpose of our lives. Too often
have we fixed our eyes on the earth and rarely have we lifted them to the stars. May we
find thee and keep thee with us every day.
Through Jesus Christ our Lord. Amen.

Vashti, the modest

Mine honor is my life: both grow in one.
Take honor from me and my life is done.
—AUTHOR UNKNOWN

Vashti means "fair, lovely."
SCRIPTURE STORY: Esther 1:9-22.
SCRIPTURE READING: Proverbs 22:1-2.
HYMNS: "I Would Be True."
"Take Time to Be Holy."

MEDITATION:

Vashti was the favorite wife of King
Ahasuerus of Persia. She was very beautiful, and the king was proud of her. As it
was customary for women to be veiled before those not in her family, very few had
seen her loveliness.

One night the king, drunken and being
urged by his courtiers, sent for Vashti to be
brought, in royal raiment, to his banquet
table, that all might admire her. Vashti,
who was accustomed to obey his slightest
whim, refused to go. Womanly and mod-

est, she decided that death was preferable to the indignity of appearing before this lewd assembly.

On receiving her reply, the king was astonished. His courtiers persuaded him that she had committed an unpardonable sin. They said that they feared all women would cease to obey their husbands if the queen were permitted to do so. They so added fuel to his wrath that he sent her out of the kingdom in dishonor and gave her belongings to another.

We may think the life of Vashti of little importance. However, Vashti stands for that womanly quality, true modesty, which was so rarely found in her day, when women were but playthings of men.

HEROISM

It takes great strength to live where you belong
When other people think that you are wrong;
People you love, and who love you, and whose
Approval is a pleasure you would choose.
To bear this pressure and succeed at length
In living your belief—well, it takes
    strength. . . . .
It takes great love to stir the human heart

To live beyond the others and apart.
A love that is not shallow, is not small,
Is not for one or two, but for them all.
                    —CHARLOTTE PERKINS GILMAN

PRAYER:

Father of all the ages, we thank thee for
the purity and modesty of this great woman
from the distant past. She has blazed a
trail which has been followed by innumer-
able of her sisters even unto the present day.
May we prize highly the womanly virtues
which thou dost exalt. Let us not parade
our virtues, condemning others who claim
nothing for themselves. Rather let us be
kindly and patient, forgiving and helpful to
those who would seek thee. In Jesus' name
and for his sake. Amen.

I will follow the upward road today.
I will keep my face to the light.
I will think high thoughts as I go my way.
I will do what I know is right.

I will look for the flowers by the side of the road.
I will laugh and love and be strong.
I will try to lighten another's load
This day as I fare along.
                    —MARY S. EDGAR